EXPERIMENTS with MATERIALS

Contents

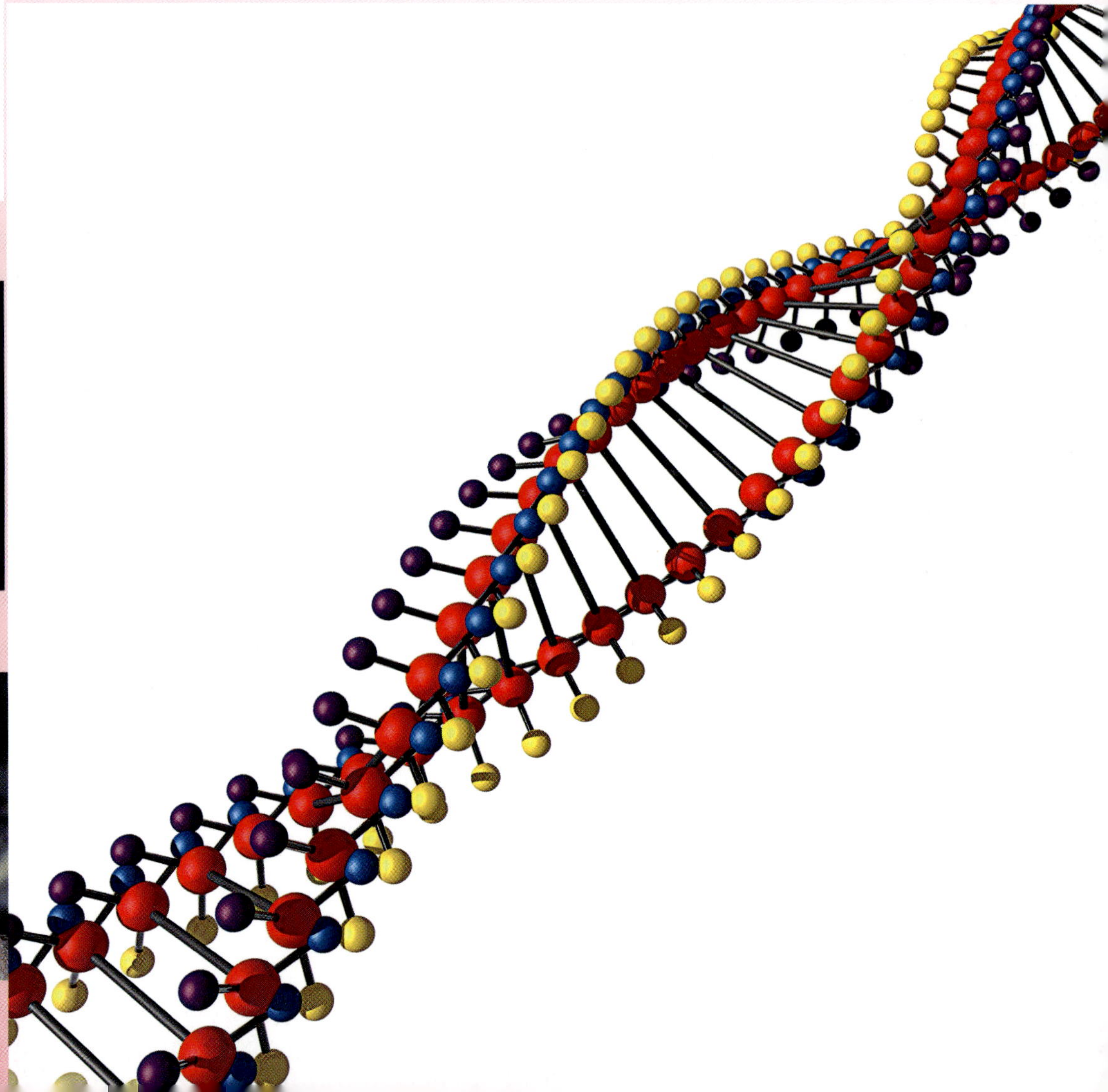

Properties of Materials

Every material you see in this world has some characteristics by which you can describe it. For example, salt is a white powder and water is a transparent liquid in which salt dissolves. Iron is a heavy and hard metal which is magnetic. Iron rusts when it reacts with water.

The above paragraph describes certain physical properties like colour, hardness, texture and also the chemical properties of some materials.

It is essential to know the physical and chemical properties of materials in order to use them properly. In this book we will explore some important physical properties of materials. This will help you appreciate why different substances behave the way they do.

To start with

1. Collect 10 different materials from around you.
2. Describe their physical properties. Be as exact as you can be – do not just say that something is heavy, but specify that it is heavier than one thing and lighter than another.
3. Try to identify groups of substances with similar physical properties. The table given on the next page might be of help to you.

Properties

Solidity		Is it a solid, a liquid or a gas?
Appearance		What colour is it? Is it shiny or dull? Is it opaque or transparent?
Texture		Is it rough or smooth?
Density		How heavy is it?
Plasticity		Can it be stretched or bent?
Brittleness		Does it break rather than bend?
Elasticity		Does it go back to its original shape after stretching?
Hardness		How hard is it? What leaves a scratch on it?
Viscosity		Does the liquid flow easily?
Solubility		Does it dissolve in water?
Magnetism		Is it magnetic?
Heat Conductivity		Does it conduct heat?

By now you must be wondering what causes such variation in materials. For an answer, you must first know what everything is made up of.

What is Everything Made of?

The thing of which all materials are made is called *matter*. It can be a solid, such as iron or wood, a liquid, such as water or kerosene, or a gas, such as air or oxygen.

Is all matter made of the same constituents? This question has bothered people for thousands of years.

Over 2,500 years ago, ancient Greek and Indian philosophers thought that all matter could be divided into four basic types or elements — earth, water, air and fire.

Many Greek thinkers, such as Aristotle, also believed that matter was really made of one continuous substance, which could be endlessly divided into smaller and smaller parts.

Other Greek thinkers, such as Democritus, however argued that matter was made of very tiny particles which cannot be seen. These particles are different in form for different bodies. As they cannot be divided further, Democritus called them atoms (from the Greek word *atomos* meaning 'indivisible').

An Indian philosopher, Kanada, had independently proposed the idea of the atom in the 6th century BC. He said that matter could not be divided into smaller and smaller particles without end. The smallest, invisible, indestructible particle of matter was termed 'Paramanu' (from the Sanskrit word meaning 'the smallest particle').

It is a pity that the Greeks found Aristotle's views on matter more convincing than those of Democritus. So the remarkable idea of the atom remained forgotten for long.

Elements and compounds

It was not until the 17th century that the theory of four elements was really challenged. In 1661 in England, Robert Boyle suggested the idea of basic pure chemicals or elements. Elements are the basic building blocks which can be combined specifically to make all other materials in the world.

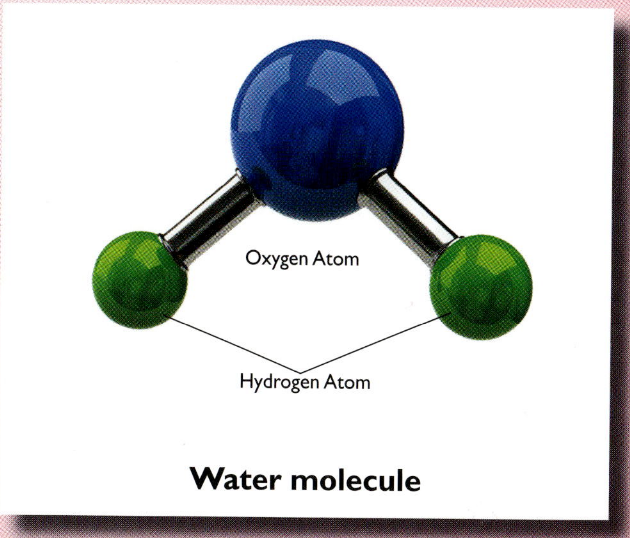

Water molecule

Soon many experiments showed that Boyle was right. New elements were discovered. Two scientists, Joseph Priestley and Antoine Lavoisier found that one of Aristotle's basic elements – air – was actually a mixture of different gases. Lavoisier also found that water was actually a chemical combination of two elements: hydrogen and oxygen. Such substances were termed compounds.

It was established that all materials are either pure elements (like iron, magnesium, sulphur, carbon, oxygen nitrogen, etc) or compounds made of these pure elements. Water, carbon dioxide, salt and glass are examples of compounds. Certain materials are just a mixture of one or both.

Try this

Make a list of all the materials you can find in your classroom. Classify them as elements, compounds and mixtures.

So far, 105 different elements have been discovered. Of these, 92 are naturally occurring elements. Only two among these 92 are liquids at ordinary temperatures. They are bromine and mercury. Only 11 elements are gases. All others are solids, mostly metals.

The *Periodic table* given on the next page gives the names of all the elements. The table was devised by a Russian scientist, Dmitri Mendeleev. It shows that all elements can be arranged in order of the increasing atomic numbers.

PERIODIC TABLE OF THE ELEMENTS

The elements	Symbol	Atomic number		Symbol	Atomic number	Atomic Symbol		Atomic number
Actinium	AC	89	Hafnium	Hf	72	Praseodyminum	Pr	59
Aluminium	Al	13	Helium	He	2	Prometheum	Pm	61
Americium	Am	95	Holmium	H0	67	Protactinium	Pa	91
Antimony	Sb	51	Hydrogen	H	1	Radium	Ra	88
Argon	Ar	18	Indium	In	49	Radon	Rn	86
Arsenic	As	33	Iodine	I	53	Rhenium	Re	75
Astatine	At	85	Iridium	Ir	77	Rhodium	Rh	45
Barium	Ba	56	Iron	Fe	26	Rubidium	Rb	37
Berkelium	Bk	97	Krypton	Kr	36	Ruthenium	Ru	44
Beryllium	Be	4	Lanthanum	La	57	Samarium	Sm	62
Bismuth	Bi	83	Lawrence	Lr	103	Scandium	Sc	21
Boron	B	5	Lead	Pb	82	Selenium	Se	34
Bromine	Br	35	Lithium	Li	3	Silicon	Si	14
Cadmium	Cd	48	Lutetium	Lu	71	Silver	Ag	47
Calcium	Ca	20	Magnesium	Mg	12	Sodium	Na	11
Californium	Cf	98	Manganese	Mn	25	Strontium	Sr	38
Carbon	C	6	Mendelevium	Md	101	Sulfur	S	16
Cerium	Ce	58	Mercury	Hg	80	Tantalum	Ta	73
Caesium	Cs	55	Molybdenum	Mo	42	Technetium	Tc	43
Chlorine	Cl	17	Neodymium	Nd	60	Tellurium	Te	52
Chromium	Cr	24	Neon	Ne	10	Terbium	Tb	65
Cobalt	Co	27	Neptunium	Np	93	Thallium	Tl	81
Copper	Cu	29	Nickel	Ni	28	Thorium	Th	90
Curium	Cm	96	Niobium	Nb	41	Thulium	Tm	69
Dysprosium	Dy	66	Nitrogen	N	7	Tin	Sn	50
Einsteinium	Es	99	Nobelium	No	102	Titanium	Ti	22
Erbium	Er	68	Osmium	Os	76	Tungsten	W	74
Europium	Eu	63	Oxygen	O	8	Uranium	U	92
Fermium	Fm	100	Palladium	Pd	46	Vanadium	V	23
Flourine	F	9	Phosphorus	P	15	Xenon	Xe	54
Francium	Fr	87	Platinum	Pt	78	Ytterbium	Yb	70
Gadolinium	Gd	64	Plutonium	Pu	94	Yttrium	Y	39
Gallium	Ga	31	Polonium	Po	84	Zinc	Zn	30
Germanium	Ge	32	Potassium	K	19	Zirconium	Zr	40
Gold	Au	79						

The Periodic Table contains three distinct type of elements – metals, non-metals and transition elements.

Atoms and molecules

In the meanwhile, the old idea of the atom slowly gained acceptance. Ultimately in 1808, an English chemist, John Dalton, established the idea of atoms in science. He proposed that atoms are the smallest unit of matter. All the atoms of an element are identical but atoms of different elements are different. For example, iron is different from aluminium because it is made up of a different kind of atom.

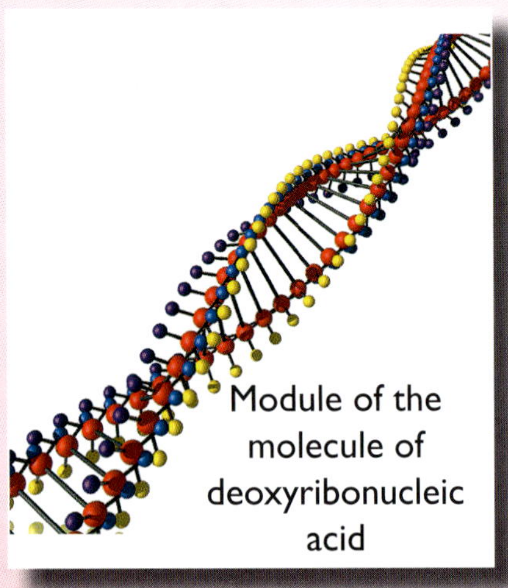

Module of the molecule of deoxyribonucleic acid

The Italian physicist, Amedio Avogadro, led the atomic theory further by showing that atoms hardly ever existed alone, but occurred in pairs. This means that the smallest unit of hydrogen gas was not an atom of hydrogen but a pair of hydrogen atoms. Moreover, atoms of one kind can pair up with atoms of another kind, only in specific combinations, to form compounds. These pairs of atoms, whether of the same kind or of different kinds, are called molecules. So we can say that all materials are made up of molecules, which in turn are made of atoms.

Did you know?

Protein molecules, the largest molecules, consist of tens and even hundreds of thousands of atoms.

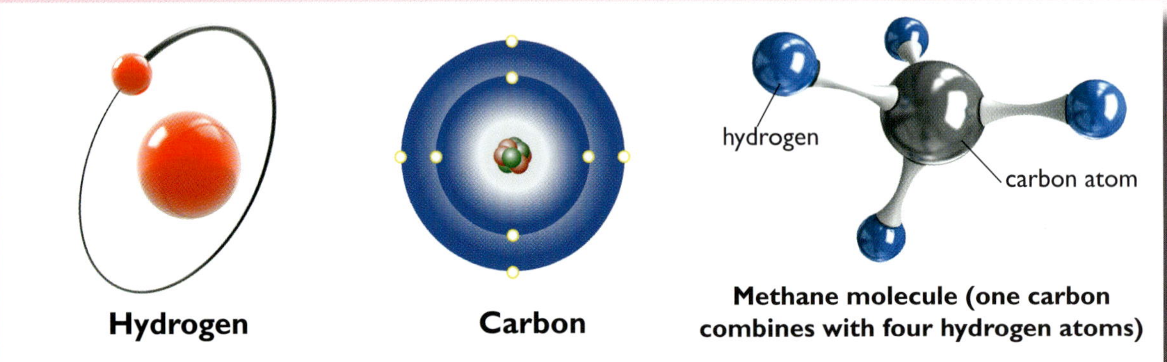

Hydrogen **Carbon** **Methane molecule (one carbon combines with four hydrogen atoms)**

Atomic structure

The indestructible atomic theory of Dalton received a blow when J.J. Thompson, while experimenting with cathode ray tubes in 1897, discovered a stream of particles 1,800 times smaller than the smallest atom. These particles were found to be electrically charged and were called *electrons*. Thompson suggested that electrons are embedded in atoms like currants in a plum pudding!

Some years later, Ernest Rutherford discovered a dense 'nucleus' at the centre of each atom with positively charged particles. These were called *protons*. Each atom of an element has a particular number of protons. This number is known as its atomic number.

According to Rutherford, the negatively charged electrons circle round a positively charged core, nucleus, in a sport of 'electron cloud'. The number of electrons and protons in an atom being the same, their charges balance out, and the atom is neutal. In 1913, the Danish scientist, Niels Bohr, suggested that the electrons circled around the nucleus in a series of orbits, in the same way as the planets orbit the sun.

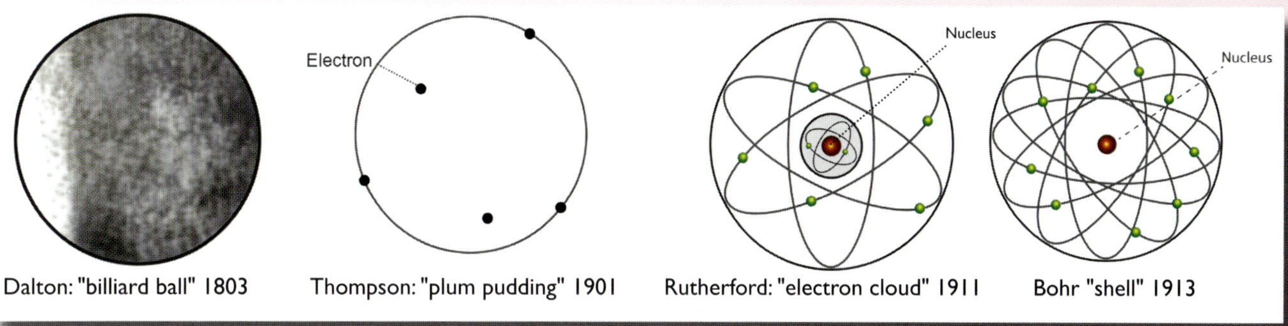

Dalton: "billiard ball" 1803 Thompson: "plum pudding" 1901 Rutherford: "electron cloud" 1911 Bohr "shell" 1913

Some years later, Chadwick discovered the presence of another particle called a *neutron* in the nucleus. Since then, scientists have discovered extremely complicated things happening inside the atom. Note that the number of electrons and their position in atoms determine the chemical behaviour of materials, while most physical properties are explained by the forces of interaction between neighbouring atoms and molecules in materials.

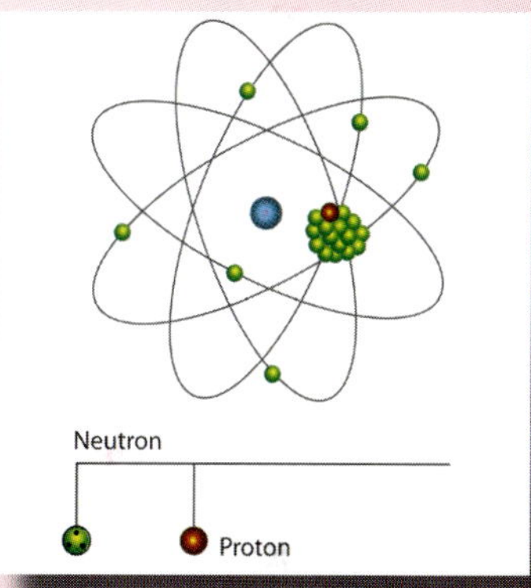

A model of atom

You will need:

- 2 thin cards of different colours
- a square board
- a pencil
- a compass
- a pair of scissors
- 36 small black beads
- large red bead
- a plastic tube
- glue

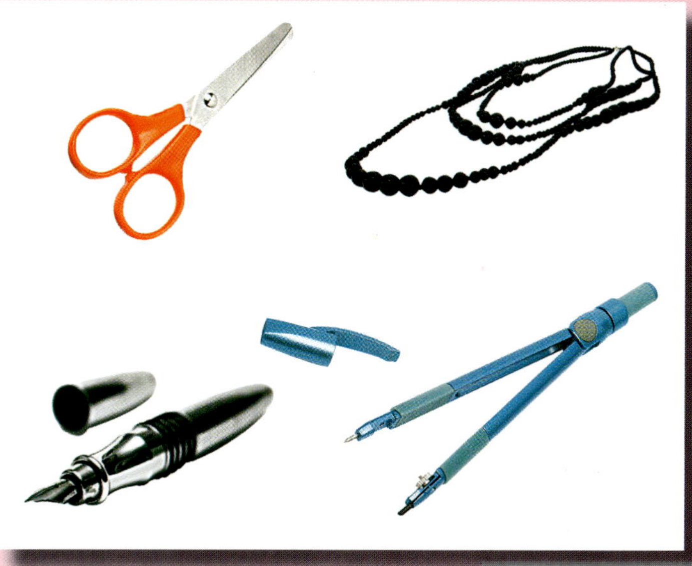

1. Draw four circles of radius 8 cm, 5 cm, 4 cm and 2 cm, respectively on the two coloured cards so that the colours alternate.
2. Paste the circles on the board, starting with the largest. The circles should be concentric. Stick one circle on top of the other.
3. Cut out 37 thin cross-sections of the plastic tube. Stick them on the circumferences of all the four circles. Place one ring in the centre, two on the circumference of the innermost circle, eight on the second, 18 on the third and 8 on the outer circle.
4. Put the red bead on the ring in the centre. This is your nucleus.
5. To represent any element, check its atomic number from the periodic table. This will tell you how many black beads are needed for electrons. Arrange the black beads, starting from the innermost orbit. For example, if you want to make a sodium atom, take 11 beads and place them as shown.

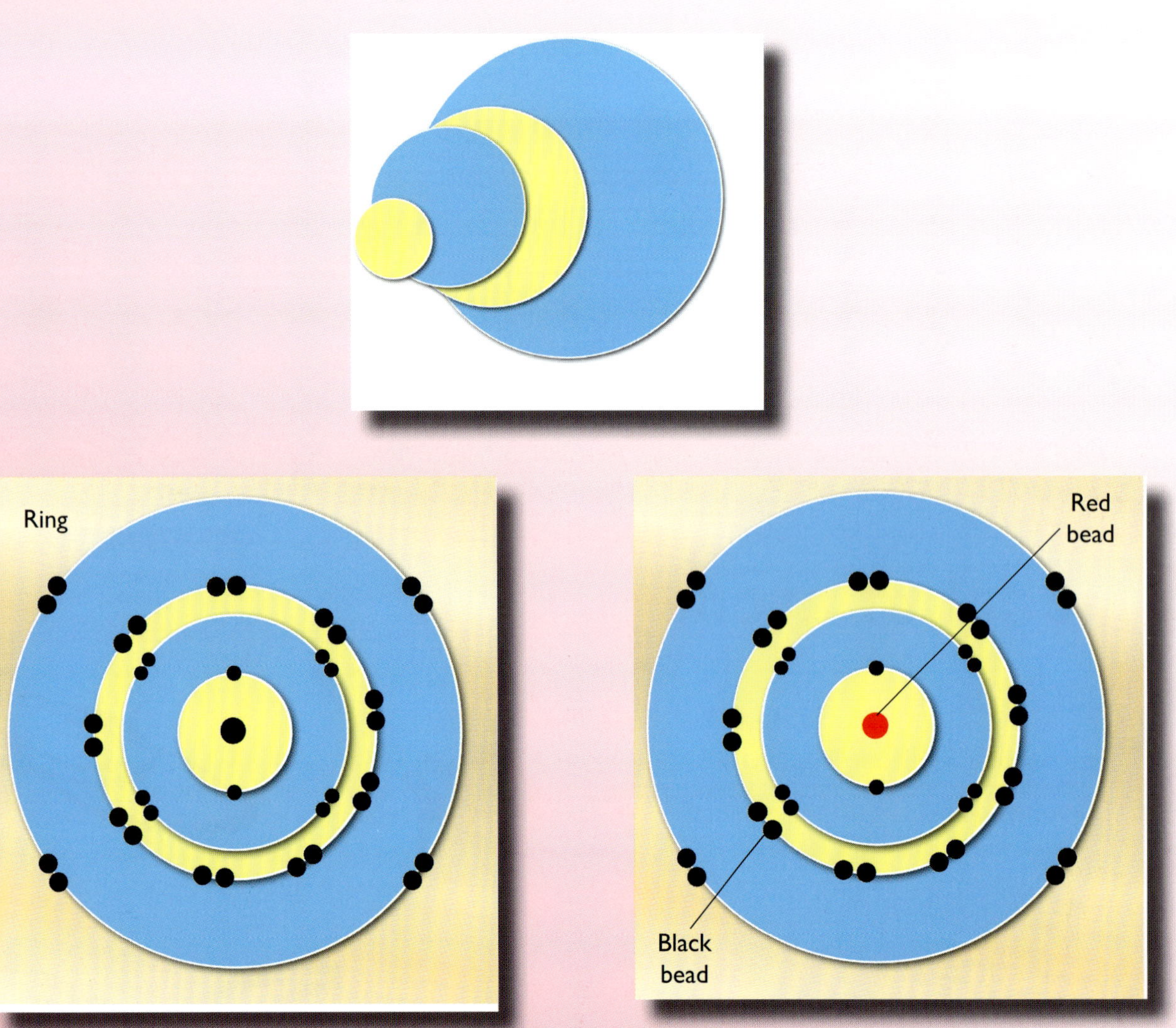

Model of Sodium atom

Solids, Liquids and Gases

All materials exist in three familiar forms or states called solids, liquids and gases. What makes a thing a solid, a liquid or a gas? To answer this, one must first know the essential difference between these three states.

A solid has a fixed shape. It is dense and rigid because the molecules which make the solid are bound tightly to one another. In other words, the force of attraction between the neighbouring molecules of a solid is strong. In the absence of this attraction, all solids would decompose into separate molecules.

But, if molecules attract each other, why can't we compress solid things easily? Does this mean that molecules of a solid cannot pull each other very close or that after a certain closeness molecules repel each other?

In reality, there is an equilibrium distance at which molecules of a solid settle down with respect to one another. This distance varies from one solid to another. For example, a solid which expands more when heated has a weaker force of attraction.

Solid

The molecules in a solid vibrate continuously about their mean position. This motion is due to the heat contained in the body. So it is called thermal motion. The speed of thermal motion increases as the solid is heated.

In a liquid, the force of attraction between molecules is weaker. So the molecules are not so rigidly bound to their neighbours. They slowly move about through the volume of the liquid like you would through a crowd. That is why liquids have no shape of their own but take the shape of the container in which they are kept. You can easily see the molecular movement in liquids.

Liquid

Try this

Take a glass of water. When the water is still, place a drop of ink carefully on the surface of the water. The ink will slowly spread through the water due to the movement of the molecules.

Since molecules in a liquid move about, there have to be empty spaces in the liquid. This means that the molecules of a liquid are loosely packed as compared to those of solids. You can verify this easily.

You will need:

- a measuring cylinder
- salt
- water

1. Half-fill the measuring cylinder with water. Note the level of the water.
2. Add salt to the water and stir gently. Is there any increase in the level of the water? Where does the salt vanish?

The salt particles dissolve in water and get adjusted in the empty spaces in water.

Unlike solids and liquids, gases have neither a fixed shape nor a fixed volume. The force of attraction between the molecules of a gas is very weak. So they move about almost like free particles and fill the whole container.

Smell the perfume

1. Spray a little perfume in one corner of a room. How long does it take before you can smell the perfume from the other corner of the room? How does the perfume spread?
2. Try the same thing with burning incense. Since the incense burns continuously the smell spreads faster and remains for a longer time.

All molecules of a gas are in a state of constant thermal motion. They collide with each other and with the walls of the container. This zigzag thermal motion is called Brownian motion (after Rober Brown who, in 1827, first noticed this 'constant oscillatory motion' in pollen grains suspended in water). You can observe the Brownian motion.

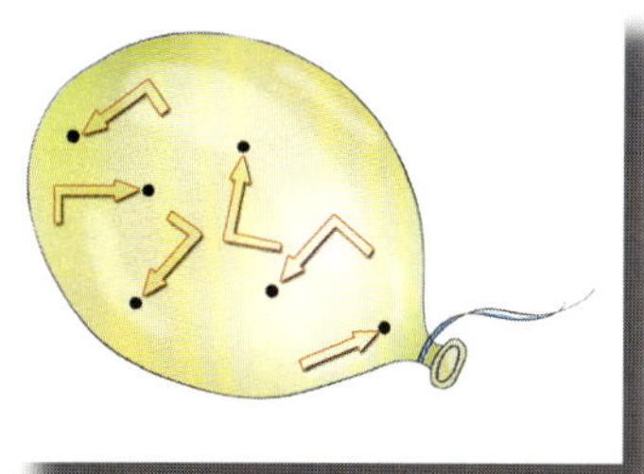

Each time a molecule hits the wall of the container, a pressure is exerted on the wall. The total pressure of a gas depends on the number of such collisions per second. You can understand that more molecules in a given volume mean more collisions, and so, more pressure.

Did you know?

One of the first scientists to study the connection between the volume of a gas and its pressure was Robert Boyle. In 1662, he showed that the product of the pressure and the volume of a given mass of gas is constant as long as the temperature does not change. This is called Boyle's law.

A change from one state to another

What is strange about the following: solid carbon dioxide, liquid oxygen and sodium vapour?

You might say that carbon dioxide and oxygen are gases, not solids or liquids while sodium is a solid, not a gas. But under what conditions are they solids, liquids or gases? You must remember that the state of a substance is determined by two things – temperature and pressure. We live in a condition where the atmospheric temperature and pressure do not vary much, and so our perception of things is as they exist under 'ordinary temperature and pressure'.

By lowering the temperature sufficiently, carbon dioxide can become a solid and oxygen, a liquid.

Solid carbon dioxide is used to form clouds of mist on the stage. Liquid oxygen is used as fuel mixture for launching rockets.

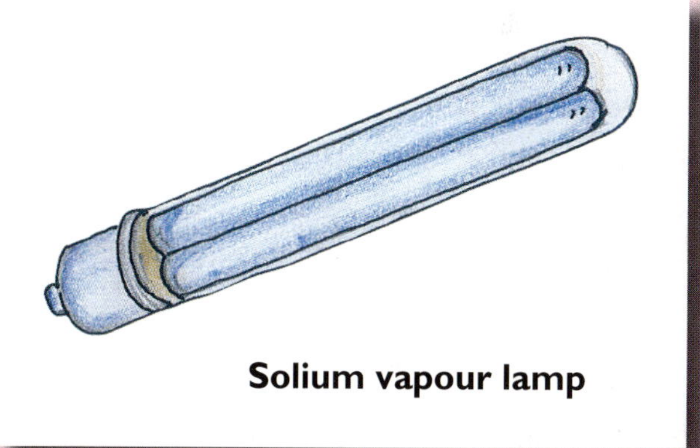

Solium vapour lamp

Sodium gets vaporised when heated. You must have seen sodium vapour lamps.
So, we find, that given the right conditions, all substances can be obtained in the three states of matter.

Melting point

Every solid turns to liquid at a certain temperature, called its *melting point*. Try measuring the melting point of some substances.

(*Remember* in certain cases you will not succeed in reaching the melting point – the solid may chemically decompose.)

You will need:

- a test tube
- butter, wax, chocolate, sugar
- a pair of tongs
- a pan or beaker
- water
- a thermometer
- a heater or gas stove

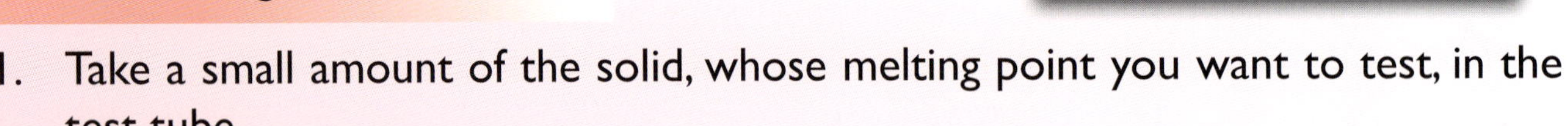

1. Take a small amount of the solid, whose melting point you want to test, in the test tube.
2. Take some water in the pan and put it on a low fire.
3. Hold the test tube with the tongs and dip it into water. Keep on shaking it gently.
4. The moment the solid starts melting, remove the tube from the water.
5. Check the temperature of the water.
6. Perform the experiment twice for each solid.
7. What does the melting point of a solid tell you about the force of attraction between its atoms and molecules?

Under pressure

Not only heat, but pressure also melts solids. You can check this as follows:

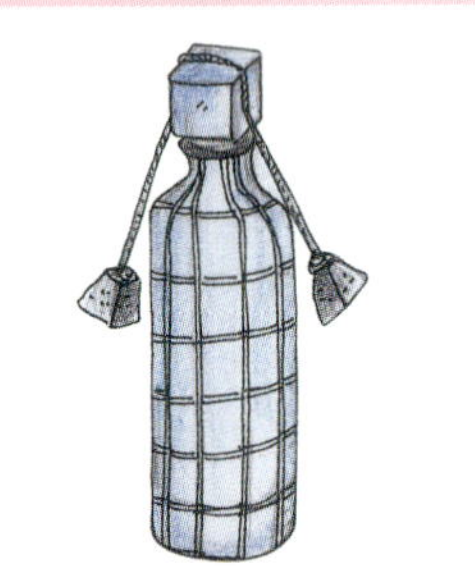

1. Tie a 250 g weight on each end of a wire.
2. Place an ice cube on the mouth of a bottle.
3. Carefully place the wire on the ice cube so that the weights hang from the sides of the bottle.
4. The wire slowly cuts through the ice. But the ice cube remains intact. How does this happen?

The pressure applied by the weights helps to melt ice below the wire. As the wire moves down, the water on top freezes back to ice.

The molecules of a solid are more densely packed

When liquids cool, they solidify. Do materials in the solid state take up less space than in the liquid state? Let's check.

You will need:

- some butter
- a thick-bottomed pan
- a small jar
- a heater

1. Heat the butter gently in the pan.
2. Remove it from the heat when it melts.
3. Pour the butter into the small jar. Fill it to the brim and put it in the refrigerator to cool.
4. Take the jar out when the butter solidifies. You will notice a deep hole in the butter. Why?

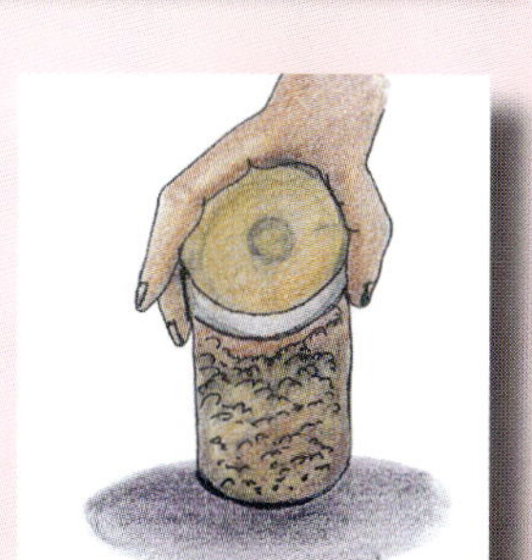

Try this

Does the same thing happen to water? Fill a plastic bottle with water. Put the bottle in a freezer and observe.**

Evaporation

When a liquid is heated, the molecules move around faster. This increases the flow of the liquid. Eventually, some of the molecules manage to overcome the force of attraction and leave the liquid surface as vapour. This is called evaporation. Evaporation takes place from the surface of a liquid at all temperatures. But the rate of evaporation increases with temperature.

1. Take two saucers. Pour a spoonful of water in each.
2. Place one saucer in the sunlight and the other in a cool, dark place.
3. Water from the first saucer will evaporate faster. Can you say why?

Arrange the following liquids in order of their evaporation rates:

1. Water   2. Eau-de-cologne   3. Ether   4. Mercury

**The bottle will crack when the water freezes inside it. Ice occupies more space than the same amount of water.

Evaporation of solids

When we say that a substance is evaporating, we usually mean that a liquid is evaporating, but solids can also evaporate. When solid directly changes from solid state to gaseous state or when the gas directly changes into a solid without passing through the liquid state is called *sublimation*.

1. Keep some naphthalene balls inside a piece of cloth.
2. Take them out after some days. The cloth will smell strongly of naphthalene. What causes the odour? The odour is caused by the molecules which break away from the naphthalene balls. Naphthalene evaporates at room temperature.
3. Check the size of the balls. Do they look smaller?

Did you know?

Every solid with an odour sublimates to a significant degree; otherwise how would you get the smell?

Boiling

A liquid boils when heated sufficiently. This happens at a particular temperature called the boiling point of the liquid. Note that the boiling point is not the point at which a liquid turns into a gas; it is the highest temperature the liquid can reach. Once this temperature is reached, a liquid cannot get any hotter. The extra heat helps to free the liquid molecules to form gas or vapour.

1. Lower a thermometer into a kettle of water.
2. Put the water to boil.
3. Watch the mercury level of the thermometer. The level of mercury starts rising immediately and soon reaches $100^{\circ}C$.
4. Note that as the water boils the mercury stops rising. The point at which the mercury stops rising is the boiling point of water.

Boil water by reducing the pressure

1. Secure a round bottomed flask with a tight stopper.

2. Half fill it with water.
3. Put it on a flame and bring the water to boil.
4. Put a stopper on its mouth and invert the flask carefully over a trough or basin.
5. Ask a friend to pour cold water over the flask. Watch the surface of the water. The water will start boiling because of the fall in air pressure inside the flask as it is cooled. When pressure is reduced, water boils at a lower temperature.

Condensation

A gas or vapour can be condensed into its liquid state by lowering its temperature. Most gases need extremely low temperatures to liquefy. Water vapour can however be liquefied or condensed at ordinary temperatures.

1. Boil a kettle of water.
2. Wrap a napkin around the handle of a spoon and, hold it in the path of the steam. Drops of water will collect on the surface of the spoon.

Did you know?

Clouds form when evaporated water from rivers and seas rises up, cools and condenses around tiny dust particles in the air.

In fact, any alien particle in the air helps condensation. You can check this.

1. Take a wide-mouthed glass jar. Pour an inch of water into it.
2. Cut up a large balloon and cover the mouth of the jar with it. Keep it in place with a book. Leave it covered for ten minutes.
3. Put some chalk dust into the jar and quickly secure the rubber sheet tightly over the mouth of the jar with a rubber band.
4. Push your fist firmly against the rubber sheet. This will warm the air inside the jar.
5. After ten seconds, quickly remove your fist. This will suddenly cool the air. Cold air can hold less water vapour than warm air. The extra water will condense around the particles of chalk dust and you will see a cloud in the jar.

The Structure of Solids

Most inorganic or non-living solids are made up of crystals which are pieces of material that have flat surfaces with straight edges. All crystals of the same substance have the same shape though they may differ in size. Salt, sugar, snowflakes and diamonds are familiar examples of crystals. However, solids like iron, copper and gold are also made of very tiny crystals. Such crystals can be observed only through a microscope.

Over a hundred years ago, scientists adopted a method to classify crystals on the basis of their external forms. According to this classification, all crystals can be divided into 32 forms, which in turn are grouped into six primary divisions, called *systems*. For example, crystals of salt, diamond, gold, silver, copper, iron and lead, all have a cubic structure; gems like sapphire, ruby, emerald and also ice and snow, crystallise in a hexagonal pattern. Solids which do not have a crystalline shape are called *amorphous*. The word amorphous comes from the Greek word meaning 'without form'. Glass is amorphous.

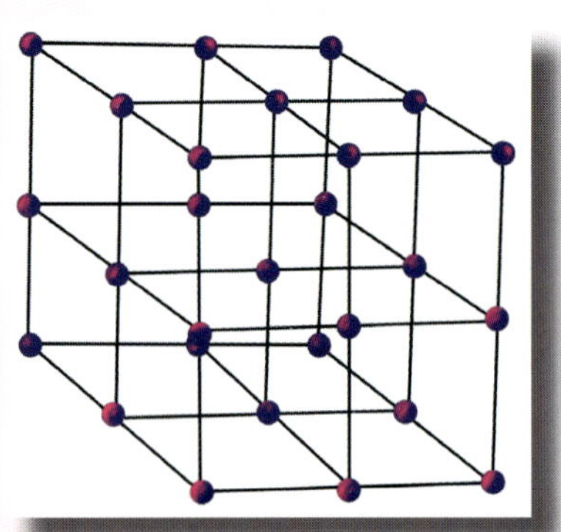

A crystal of Sodium Chloride has a cubical pattern

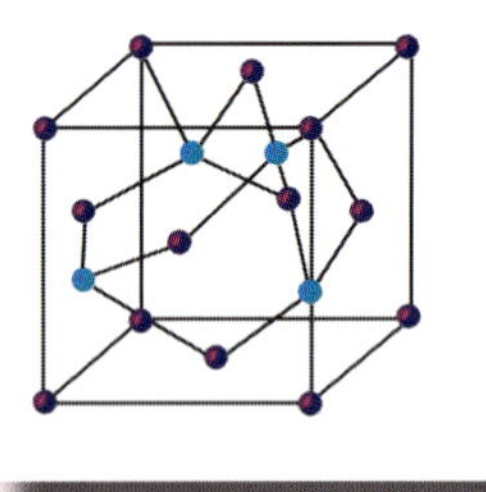

Crystal growth

Minerals become crystalline when molten mass or rocks slowly cool down as they move upwards into the earth's crust. You can very easily grow your own crystal from a solution of a substance.

1. Dissolve some salt in a glass of water. You can dissolve up to 70 g of salt in a glass of water (200 ml) at 20°C. The water will be saturated with salt. No more salt will dissolve in it.
2. Keep the saturated salt solution aside. After a few days you will find crystals of salt at the bottom. Notice that the level of the water in the glass has gone down. This is due to evaporation.

3. Throw the water away and collect the crystals on a piece of black paper. Observe the crystals under a magnifying glass.

Crystals of a solid can also be formed from its vapour

Black shiny crystals of iodine can be formed by cooling iodine vapour. Iodine passes from the gaseous to the solid state directly, without passing through the liquid state, under normal conditions of pressure.

Obtain large crystals

The process of crystallisation is greatly assisted if a tiny crystal is put into the saturated solution while making crystals. This is called a seed crystal. The seed crystal draws to itself all the material separating out of the solution, thus preventing the formation of a large number of small crystals.

Make a large crystal of sugar

You will need:

- sugar
- a glass jar
- a dish
- a piece of thread
- a card

1. First make a strong sugar solution by dissolving sugar in a jar of water.
2. Pour a little solution into the shallow dish and leave it to evaporate.
3. After four-five days you will find many crystals in the dish.
4. Select the largest crystal and tie it to a thread. This will act as a seed for crystallisation.
5. Tie the thread to a card and suspend it in the jar.
6. After two weeks, take out your crystal. How big is it?

Why do we need large crystals?

Science laboratories and industries are often in need of large crystals in which the crystal growth is not haphazard. The optical industry needs large crystals of calcite, rock salt, fluorite, etc. Crystals of ruby, sapphire and certain other precious stones are used as bearings in the watch-making industry. Quartz is widely employed because of its property of transforming mechanical pressure into electrical voltage.

What makes a crystal?

Crystals are made of a regular arrangement of atoms or molecules. In fact, this arrangement or pattern determines the properties of a solid, like hardness, melting point, and heat and electrical conductivity.

For example, carbon, which occurs in two very different forms. One form, which is the diamond, is a very hard material. The hardness results from the very strong bonds between the atoms in a diamond crystal. The other form, graphite, is one of the softest substances. It has a structure in which the carbon atoms lie in layers. There are only weak links between the layers. As a result, graphite is a relatively weak material, used as a lubricant. Graphite conducts electricity, but diamond does not!

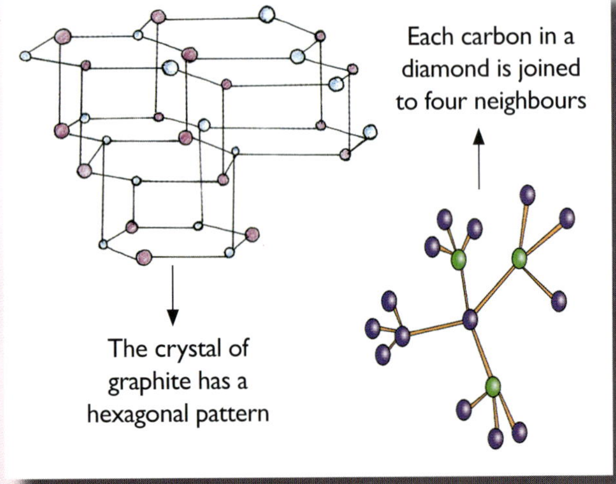

The possession of a definite melting point is an important feature of crystalline solids. Tungsten has the highest melting point of 3380^{0}C. That is why it is used widely in filaments of electric bulbs. Iron melts at 1539^{0}C, gold at 1063^{0}C, mercury at -39^{0}C, etc.

Amorphous substances

In contrast to crystals, amorphous solids like glass and obsidian do not have a definite melting point. These substances do not form crystals. Their inner and outer structure is haphazard and shapeless. When a piece of hard glass is heated, it becomes soft and can be easily stretched or bent. You can check this easily.

1. Hold a glass tube over a Bunsen burner flame so that only the middle part gets heated.
2. After a while, gently pull the tube outwards. The softened glass will stretch easily.
3. Remove the tube from the heat and check the shape.

Strength of Solids

The strength of a solid is its capacity to withstand a force applied to change its shape or volume. This capacity of a solid depends on the arrangement of the atoms and molecules in its crystals. All solids yield somewhat on forces applied to them. But they react differently to different kinds of forces.

You will need:

- a plasticine ball
- a rubber band
- a piece of paper
- a piece of iron
- a piece of glass

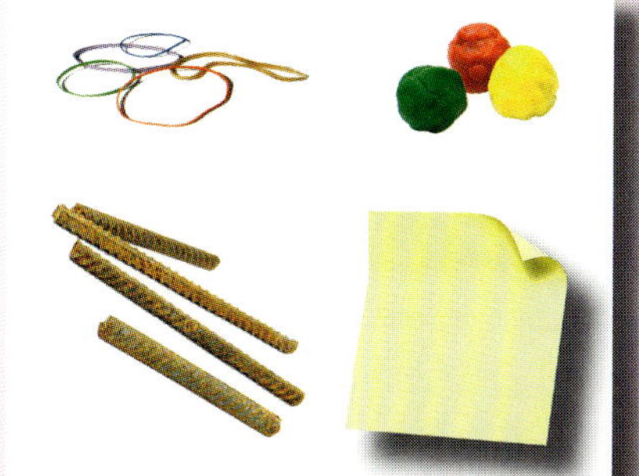

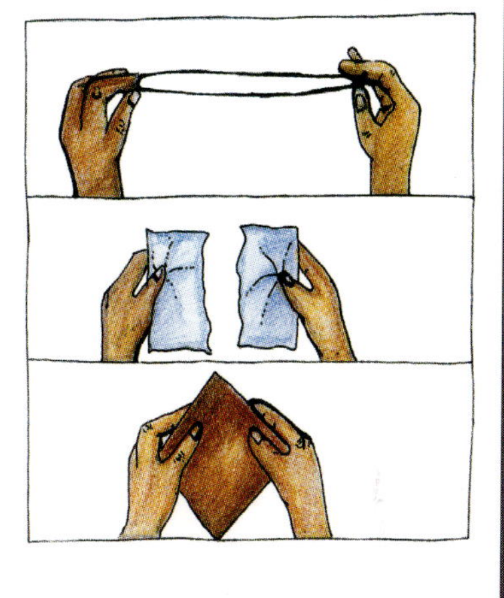

1. Hammer the five substances. The plasticine ball gets deformed. The glass breaks. Nothing happens to the rubber band, the paper and the piece of iron.
2. Pull all the five things with both hands. The rubber band stretches when pulled but jumps back to its original shape and size when you stop pulling. It is elastic. Nothing of this sort happens to glass, paper or iron. Are they not elastic? Plasticine, when pulled, stretches, but it fails to regain its original shape. Is it inelastic?
3. Try tearing these objects. You can tear the paper. Why?

From the above observations you can understand the need for classifying objects as elastic, inelastic, plastic, hard, brittle and so on, depending upon their behaviour under different kinds of load.

Elasticity

Elasticity is the ability of a body to recover its form after a force ceases to act on it. Rubber is elastic because it regains its shape and size after being stretched or compressed. So are iron and steel. That is why a spring balance is made of coiled iron spring.

Putty and plasticine are not elastic because they do not go back to their original shape. Copper and aluminium are less elastic than steel and glass but more elastic than putty and plasticine.

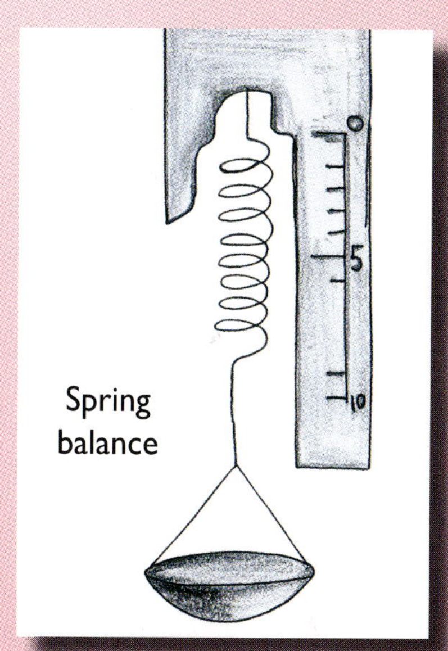

Spring balance

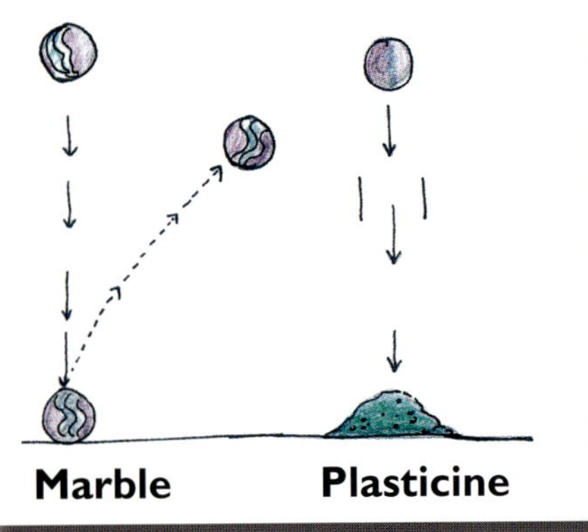

1. One way of finding out how elastic things are is by bouncing them off a hard floor.
2. Get the materials to be tested in the form of same sized balls.
3. Drop the items one by one from the same height and measure the height to which they bounce. A marble, for instance will rise quite high. It is elastic. But a plasticine ball will simply get flattened. It is inelastic.

Another way of checking elasticity is by hanging known weights from rods of different materials, measuring the change in length, and then removing the weights to see if the rods regain their original lengths. The problem with this experiment is that the elongation produced by readily available weights in most cases will be very small.

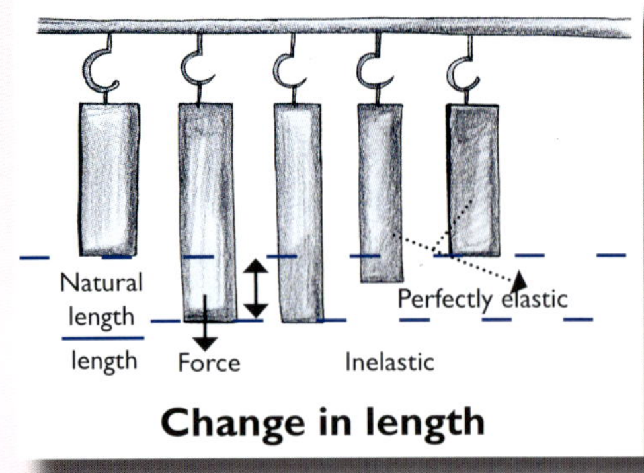

Change in length

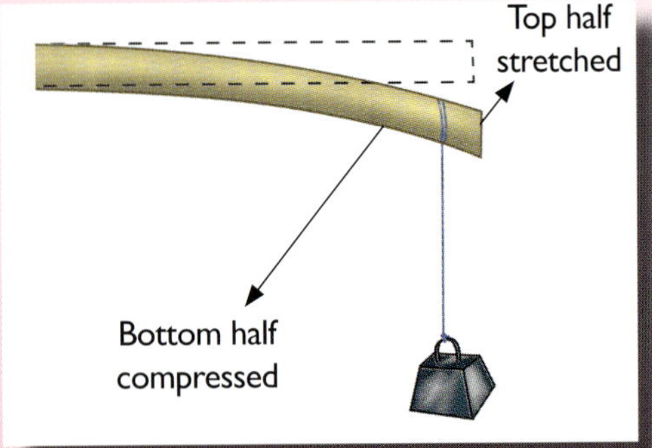

Elasticity can be checked in other ways too. Squeezing a piece of rubber makes it smaller. This is called compression. You can bend a wooden ruler by applying a small amount of pressure. Bending is a combination of stretching and compressing. If you bend a ruler downwards, the top surface is compressed.

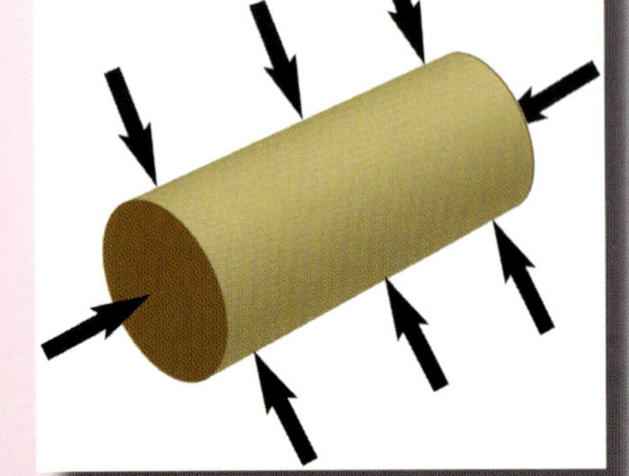

The force acting on a unit area of a solid which causes a change or distortion is called stress. When a body is under stress, a strain develops in it. The simplest kind of distortion or strain is a change in length, or tensile strain. Among other strains are compressive strain and volume strain (a change in volume).

Try this

Choose a dictionary or any other thick book. Keep it on a table and push the top of the book horizontally. The pages will slide in the direction of the force. What kind of strain does this force produce?

The force changes the shape of the book without changing its size. This is called a shearing strain.

In the 17th century, an English scientist, Robert Hooke, investigated the properties of solids under stress, and found that for an elastic substance, the strain produced on a body is proportional to the stress applied. This is called Hooke's Law.

Solids are strange!

Glass, which is brittle at low temperatures, becomes plastic at higher temperatures. It can then be blown and shaped.

Iron, which is very hard at low temperatures, behaves like a plastic at high temperatures and hence can be forged easily.

Iron forging

Clay is plastic when wet. It is stony and hard when dry. But when clay is heated to a high temperature (baked) to make bricks and ceramics, it no longer remains plastic when wet.

This behaviour of solids will not seem strange if you remember that the packing of atoms in solids changes with temperature.

Strength and hardness do not go hand in hand. Hardness is the resistance to penetration. A body is hard if it is difficult to scratch it and difficult to leave an imprint on it.

Testing for hardness

Ten minerals are arranged in order of hardness, so that each one on the scale can scratch the one before it and can be scratched by the one after it. Diamond (10), for example, is the hardest substance in the world. The softest mineral, talc, has the least hardness.

Can you tell the hardness of a mineral that can be scratched by quartz, and the mineral that leaves its mark on feldspar?

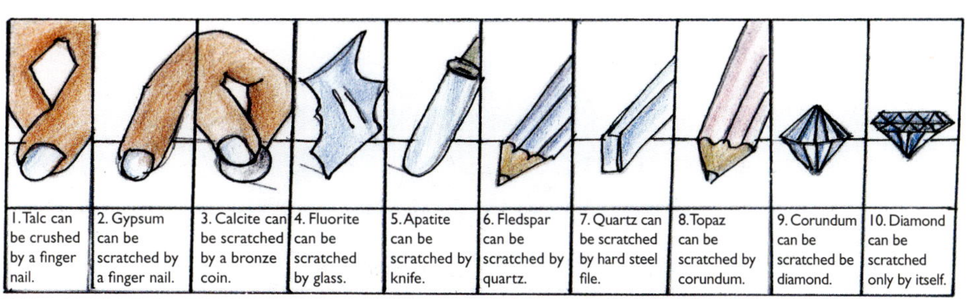

Floating and Sinking

We all know that certain things float on water while others sink. An object that floats on water might sink in alcohol, and one that sinks in water might float on glycerine. What is the reason for this?

Things that float on water are lighter or less dense than water; things that sink are heavier or denser than water. When any object is immersed in water, its weight pushes down. The water in turn pushes back upwards with a force called '*upthrust*'. Now, the question is, who wins?

Let's check

You will need:

- a brick
- a block of wood
- a trough of water

1. Lower the brick into the water. The brick sinks because its density is more than that of water. The upthrust is less than its weight.
2. Lower the block of wood into water. It floats. Wood is less dense than water.
3. Push the wood to the bottom of the water. Can you feel the upthrust pushing against your hand?
4. Let the wood go. It bobs up and floats on the water. It floats at a level at which the upthrust just equals its weight.

Try this

Iron is denser than water. Then how do ships made of iron float?

Why things float

Archimedes, an ancient Greek scientist, was the first to study upthrusts. He found that a body immersed wholly or partly in a fluid (meaning liquids and gases) is buoyed upward with an upthrust equal to the weight of the fluid it displaces. This principle, which explains buoyancy, is called *Archimedes' Principle*. It means that if an object pushes aside (displaces) one kg of water, then there will be an upthrust of 1 kg acting on the object.

A body can float only when the weight of the liquid it displaces is more than its own weight. So dense substances, like iron, can also be made to float by reshaping them to increase the volume of the water they displace, thereby increasing the *upthrust*.

Make a plasticine boat

You will need:

- a bucket three-fourths full of water
- plasticine

1. Make a ball of the plasticine.
2. Drop it gently into the water. The ball sinks because it is denser than water. Mark the raised water level.
3. Take out the ball and reshape it into a boat.
4. Place the boat on the water. Does it float? Note the water level again. Why is it higher than the previous mark? A greater volume of water is displaced by the boat and the air that it holds.
5. Change the shape of the boat. Note that the boat will always sink to such a depth that the weight of the displaced water is the same as its own weight.

Let's measure buoyancy

You will need:

- weighing scales
- a glass jar
- a small container that will float
- a large dish
- water

1. Take the weighing pan off the scales and adjust the needle so that it reads zero.
2. Place the scales on the large dish.
3. Put the glass jar filled with water on the scales and and note the weight.

5. Gently place the small container on the water. Some water will spill into the dish. Note the weight again. Why is there no increase in weight because of the container?
6. The weight of the spilled water must be the same as that of the floating container. Verify this as follows.
7. Carefully lift the jar off the scales. Take the container out and wipe it dry.
8. Weigh the container.
9. Remove the scales from the dish. Replace the weighing pan. Reset to zero.
10. Pour the water from the dish into the pan. What is the weight of this volume of water? Is it equal to the weight of the container?

Water is buoyant

Check this when you are taking a bath.

1. Fill a bathtub with water.
2. Lie down in the tub and try to raise your whole body by pushing at the bottom of the tub with your hands. You will find this easy enough.
3. If you try to raise yourself in the same way from the living room floor, you will realise how much the buoyancy of water helped you.

A submarine works on the principle of buoyancy. A submarine's weight is normally a little less than the weight of the same volume of water. When the craft wants to go down, its tanks are filled with water, so that it now weights more than an equal volume of water, and hence it sinks. It rises by forcing the water out of the tanks.

Just as solids which are less dense than water float, so do liquids that are less dense, provided they do not mix. You can check this.

Viscosity

All liquids flow to fill up the space in which they are contained. But some liquids flow more easily than others. Oil, for example, flows more slowly than water, and honey flows still more slowly. A liquid's resistance to flow — its stickiness — is known as *viscosity.* A highly viscous liquid is one which flows slowly. We can judge the viscosity of a liquid either by the speed with which solid bodies fall in it, or by the speed with which it pours through an opening.

Test the viscosity of liquids

You will need:
- marbles
- jam jars
- test liquids — water, milk, cooking oil, alcohol, glycerine, honey and ketchup

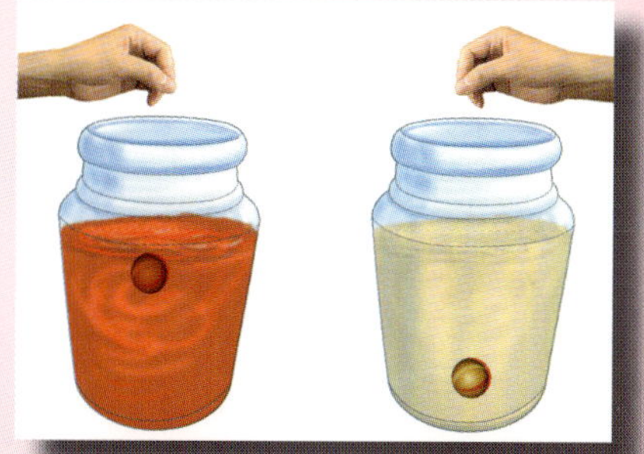

1. Fill the jam jars with equal amounts of the liquids.
2. Place the jars against a white background.
3. Ask a friend to take a marble in each hand and hold them over the first two jars.
4. The friend releases both the marbles at the same moment, while you watch them fall. Which marble reaches the bottom first? That liquid is the less viscous of the two.
5. Repeat the test, changing one liquid at a time, till you can put the liquids in order of viscosity.

Did you know?

Gases also have viscosity, but it is much less than found in liquids.

Is sealing wax a solid or a very viscous liquid?

You will need:
- 2 corks
- 2 cups
- molten sealing wax
- Molten saltpetre (potassium nitrate)

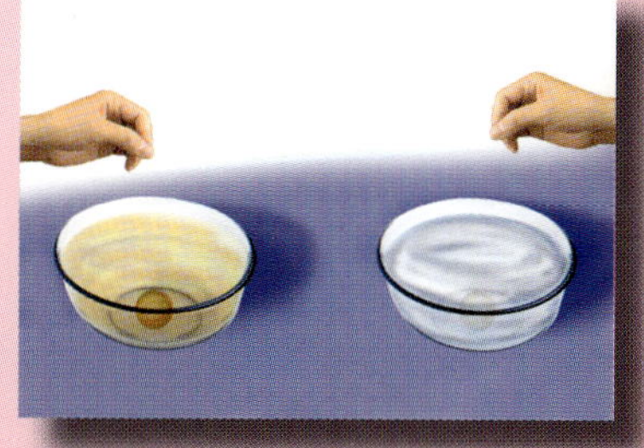

1. Place the corks at the bottom of the two cups.
2. Pour the molten wax and saltpetre into the cups respectively.
3. Both liquids will harden and bury the corks. Put the cups away in a cupboard.
4. After several months, you will observe a strange phenomenon. The cork drowned in saltpetre will be lying at the bottom, while the one drowned in sealing wax will be on the top! How did this occur? The cork came to the surface in quite the same way as it would do in water. The only difference being that of time. When the viscous force is small, a cork comes up instantly, but in very viscous liquids it may take months. Sealing wax is an amorphous substance which, as we know, resembles a liquid much more than a crystalline solid.

Liquids are stubborn

Pushing harder or moving faster through a liquid only makes the liquid resist more — the viscosity of the liquid increases. This is because pressure squeezes a liquid and the empty spaces between the molecules reduce, making it harder for them to move.

Try this

Why does heating a liquid make it less viscous?